How to

A BIG BROTHER

A Warm Story to Prepare for a New Baby Sibling

This story, adapted from children's retellings by a team of inspired parents and teachers, aims to help your child feel positive about welcoming a new baby.

Get FREE Helpful Resources at
MamTalkPublishing.com

MamTalk
BOOKS FOR KIDS

A Gift for

....

From

....

Date

....

Once upon a time, I lived happily with my Mommy and Daddy.

I loved to play ball, catch butterflies, and walk in the rain. But playing alone wasn't much fun.

One day, I told my Mommy and Daddy,
"I wish I had a brother or sister!
It's more fun to play together!"
Guess what? Yay! They agreed! By the way,
they don't always give me what I ask for!
Want to know what happened next? Then listen!

YAY!!!

My new brother or sister didn't come right away. First, the baby grew in Mommy's tummy. Her tummy got bigger every day.

Daddy and I took care of Mommy a lot.

Finally, the big day came! Daddy took Mommy to the hospital. Don't worry! Mommy is okay! She just needs the doctors' help to bring the baby into the world.

Mommy said I had to stay home with my nanny. I agreed because I wanted the baby to be born safely.

Then, we went to the hospital to bring Mommy and the baby home! We brought chocolates and flowers for Mommy and a cute stroller for the baby.

Mommy hugged me and said, "I can't believe you're so grown up. You're a big brother now! I still remember the day we brought you home for the first time."

The baby is so tiny and sweet. I realize the baby can't play with me yet. But I know my lovely new baby sibling will grow up soon.

The baby cries because newborn babies can't talk. Mommy has to take care of the baby a lot, and I want to help because I'm the big brother!

Mommy says she can't manage without me. I feel so important and helpful!

I can help my Mommy change diapers, hold the bottle, bring the pacifier, rock the crib, sing lullabies, and go for walks together.

Mommy says, "You just have to wait a little while until the baby grows up. Right now, the baby doesn't know anything and can't do much. Newborns can't even see much—only Mommy, a bottle, or a toy near the crib."
I think, "Oh, my poor darling! Little baby needs us so much!"

Mommy is right. The baby needs our help. The baby doesn't know anything about our big world yet. The baby was swimming in Mommy's tummy and suddenly arrived here. We need to help the baby feel at home!

You are the best brother in the world!

This story is **adapted from kids' retellings** by a team of **inspired parents and teachers** to help your child **feel positive about welcoming a new baby.**

We truly love helping parents and kids, and **your review can help us continue to improve and assist more families**. Thank you for choosing us!

Please take a moment **to find the book on Amazon** and share **a few words in the review section**. Your feedback is invaluable, and **we greatly appreciate your support!**

MamTalk
BOOKS FOR KIDS

MAMTALKPUBLISHING.COM/FREE

Made in the USA
Las Vegas, NV
08 January 2025